Mathematics
Grade 1

TABLE OF CONT

MW00907281

DOUBLE-DIGIT EQUATIONS & MORE WITH NUMBERS

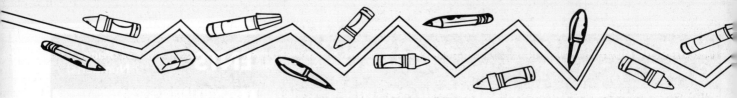

Mathematics Grade 1
Double-Digit Equations & More with Numbers

Materials You Will Need:

❑ A good pencil (or 2) with a working eraser

❑ Crayons

Check your work with the Answer Key at the back of this book!

Benefits of Math Grade 1 – Double-Digit Equations & More with Numbers:

1. Get to know the numbers 1-100.

2. Count by 10's, 5's, and 2's!

3. Practice addition & subtraction with two digits!

4. Learn to measure time, length, and more!

5. Get ready to read a calendar.

6. Understand a little bit about fractions.

Parent & Teacher Coaching Tips:

❑ *Prepare.* Provide your child with a quiet, well-lit place to study. Prepare a desk or table with an upright chair that is comfortable. Make sure that your child has plenty of room to work and spread out materials.

❑ *Schedule.* Set a study schedule. Choose a time that seems to work well for your child. Include your child in this study scheduling process and select a time when your child is well-rested and alert. Be sure to allow a break from working after a long school day.

❑ *Engage.* How does your child learn best? Use your child's learning strengths to reinforce information AND work to build new skills with your child. Encourage FUN through movement, play, acting, writing, drawing, singing, music, talking, thinking, and more while you work with your child.

❑ *Break.* Take frequent breaks from studying. Throughout the book, you will find Review Pages after each section of skills. When your child completes a section, use the Book Mark to mark your place in the book. Take a break and return to studying at your next scheduled time.

❑ *Relax!* Your role is critical in helping your child succeed with this workbook, at school, and with tests. Be sure to help your child to: eat well, sleep well, practice deep-breathing techniques to relax, visualize success, and release energy in a physical way (i.e. running, walking, playing sports).

❑ *Talk.* Encourage your child to talk about feelings related to test-anxiety, help your child understand the need for tests AND stress the value of <u>real</u> learning that is not always obvious with test scores.

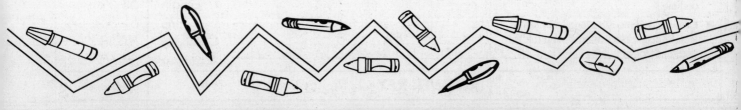

Name:_____   Date:_____

  Look at the pictures in the chart. What numbers belong there? Write the number beside each picture below.

1	2	3	4	5	6		8	9	10
11	12	13	14	15		17	18	19	20
21	22		24	25	26	27	28		30
31	32	33	34	35	36		38	39	40
	42	43	44	45	46	47	48	49	50
51	52	53		55	56	57	58	59	
61	62	63	64	65		67	68	69	70
71		73	74	75	76	77	78	79	80
81	82	83	84		86	87	88	89	90
91	92	93	94	95	96		98	99	100

 - - - - - - - - - - - - - - 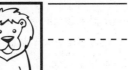 - - - - - - -  - - - - - - -

 - - - - - - - - - - - - - -  - - - - - - -  - - - - - - -

 - - - - - - - - - - - - - - - - - - - - -  - - - - - - -

Counting and writing numbers from 1 to 100

3

Draw a line from the number to the matching number word.

Challenge: On a separate sheet of paper, write the number words up to 10. Can you write any of the words for the numbers that come after 10?

1

2

3

4

5

6

7

8

9

10

three

seven

eight

ten

one

nine

two

five

four

six

Matching numbers with number words

first 1st   second 2nd   third 3rd   fourth 4th   fifth 5th   sixth 6th   seventh 7th   eighth 8th   ninth 9th   tenth 10th

Circle the toy to show the ordinal number.

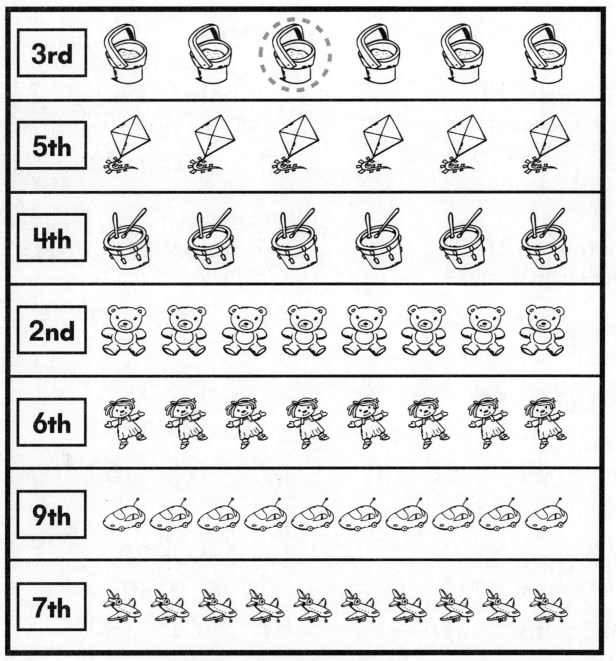

3rd

5th

4th

2nd

6th

9th

7th

Identifying and using ordinal numbers

5

25   **26   27**   28

26 comes **before 27**.

 Circle the number that comes **before**.

I am **before 37**.
What number am I?
36   **38**   **47**

I am **before 89**.
What number am I?
90   **98**   **88**

I am **before 17**.
What number am I?
16   **18**   **37**

I am **before 23**.
What number am I?
25   **24**   **22**

I am **before 50**.
What number am I?
60   **49**   **51**

I am **before 61**.
What number am I?
67   **64**   **60**

I am **before 98**.
What number am I?
100   **99**   **97**

I am **before 80**.
What number am I?
81   **79**   **90**

56   **57** → **58**   59

58 comes **after** 57.

 Write the number that comes **after**.

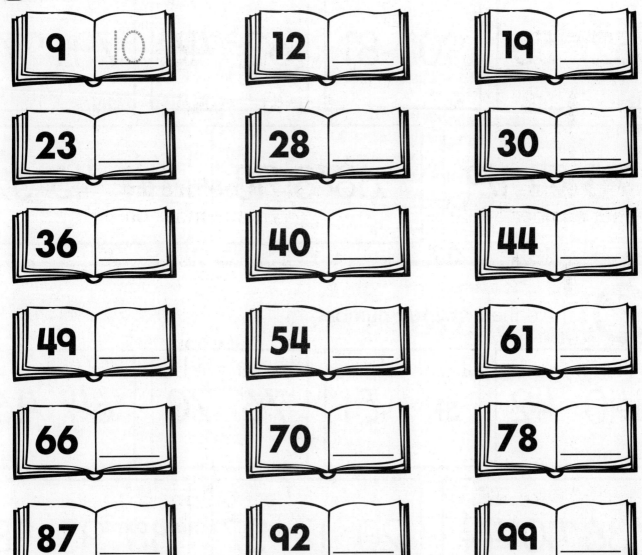

9 10	12	19
23	28	30
36	40	44
49	54	61
66	70	78
87	92	99

81 is the **larger** number.
56 is the **smaller** number.

 Challenge: Play *Larger Is Higher* with a friend. Have your friend call out a number between 1 and 100. You must call out a number that is **larger (higher)** than that number. Continue playing until you reach 100. Then, start again with a new number.

 Circle the **larger** number.

| (52) 50 | 90 81 | 63 46 | 79 97 |

| 75 71 79 | 68 78 98 | 44 45 32 |

 Circle the **smaller** number.

| (40) 42 | 31 51 | 76 78 | 64 46 |

| 36 40 44 | 20 17 27 | 88 93 98 |

Name:_____   Date:_____

Review: Numbers & Number Order

Write the missing numerals.

after	before	in between
4 _____	_____ 19	2 _____ 4
15 _____	_____ 6	11 _____ 13
8 _____	_____ 13	7 _____ 9
0 _____	_____ 2	15 _____ 17
46 _____	_____ 24	32 _____ 34
31 _____	_____ 91	59 _____ 61
76 _____	_____ 43	70 _____ 72
55 _____	_____ 65	48 _____ 50
82 _____	_____ 79	83 _____ 85
94 _____	_____ 87	25 _____ 27
1st _____	_____ 7th	9th _____ 11th
3rd _____	_____ 9th	4th _____ 6th

Name:_____   Date:_____

Review: Numbers & Number Order

 Write the number that matches the word.

two _____   **five** _____   **ten** _____

six _____   **three** _____   **nine** _____

  Circle the largest number. Draw a square around the smallest number.

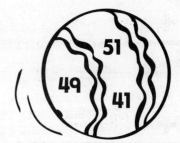

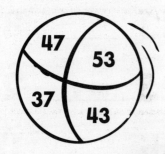
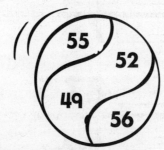

 TAKE A BREAK! You did a great job! Place your Book Mark here & RELAX!

Name:_____ Date:_____

  Add the numbers together and write the sum.

Tip: For each equation, draw your own blocks or pictures above the numbers to help you add.

4   +   4   =   8

---

4 + 6 = 10

3 + 7 = ____

1 + 5 = ____

8 + 0 = ____

6 + 3 = ____

2 + 4 = ____

7 + 2 = ____

1 + 9 = ____

5 + 5 = ____

5 + 3 = ____

4 + 3 = ____

2 + 5 = ____

Name:_____ Date:_____

  Add the numbers together and write the sum.

```
    2
+   5
─────
    7
```

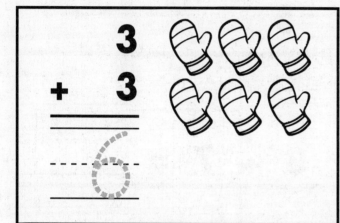

```
    3
+   3
─────

    6
```

```
    5
+   4
─────

```

```
    0
+   8
─────

```

```
    3
+   4
─────

```

```
    9
+   1
─────

```

```
    8
+   2
─────

```

```
    4
+   4
─────

```

```
    6
+   3
─────

```

Name:_____   Date:_____

  Add the numbers together and write the sum. Then, use the letter code to write in the matching letter to help solve the riddle.

9 = A	11 = S	13 = L	15 = R	17 = H
10 = F	12 = E	14 = T	16 = O	18 = N

How do basketball players stay cool at a basketball game?

9	8	6	7	4
+ 5	+ 9	+ 6	+ 8	+ 8

5	6	5
+ 4	+ 9	+ 7

5	7	6	4
+ 8	+ 9	+ 8	+ 7

8	6
+ 8	+ 4

5	3	9	3
+ 5	+ 6	+ 9	+ 8

Tip: Solve the equations first. Then, look at the code for the matching letter.

Finding sums to 18

13

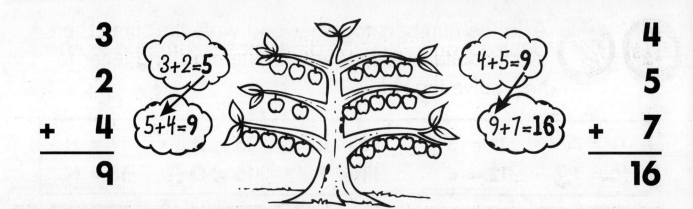

$$
\begin{array}{r} 3 \\ 2 \\ +\ 4 \\ \hline 9 \end{array}
\qquad
\begin{array}{r} 4 \\ 5 \\ +\ 7 \\ \hline 16 \end{array}
$$

 Add the three numbers together and write the sum.

$$
\begin{array}{r} 5 \\ 3 \\ +\ 6 \\ \hline \end{array}
\qquad
\begin{array}{r} 4 \\ 1 \\ +\ 9 \\ \hline \end{array}
\qquad
\begin{array}{r} 3 \\ 4 \\ +\ 8 \\ \hline \end{array}
\qquad
\begin{array}{r} 3 \\ 2 \\ +\ 7 \\ \hline \end{array}
\qquad
\begin{array}{r} 3 \\ 4 \\ +\ 5 \\ \hline \end{array}
$$

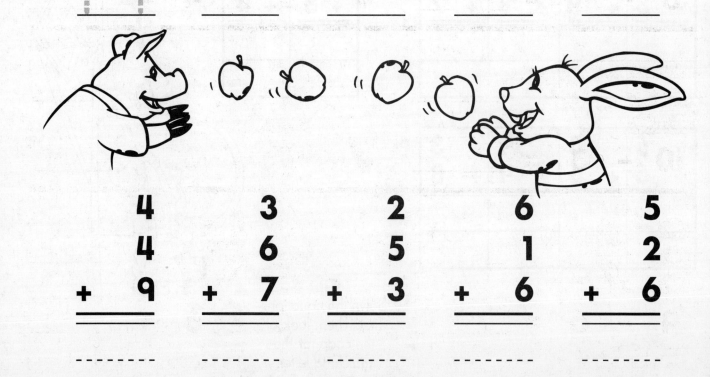

$$
\begin{array}{r} 4 \\ 4 \\ +\ 9 \\ \hline \end{array}
\qquad
\begin{array}{r} 3 \\ 6 \\ +\ 7 \\ \hline \end{array}
\qquad
\begin{array}{r} 2 \\ 5 \\ +\ 3 \\ \hline \end{array}
\qquad
\begin{array}{r} 6 \\ 1 \\ +\ 6 \\ \hline \end{array}
\qquad
\begin{array}{r} 5 \\ 2 \\ +\ 6 \\ \hline \end{array}
$$

Adding three numbers

Name:_____ Date:_____

  Subtract and write the difference. Then, add to check.

5 − 3 = __2__ ✓ 2 + 3 = __5__

9 − 5 = _____ ✓ 4 + 5 = _____

6 − 4 = _____ ✓ 2 + 4 = _____

10 − 3 = _____ ✓ 7 + 3 = _____

 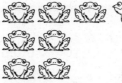

9 − 6 = _____ ✓ 3 + 6 = _____

Subtract and write the difference.

How many are left?

$14 - 8 =$ _____ 6

$13 - 6 =$ _____

$12 - 7 =$ _____

$9 - 0 =$ _____

$11 - 5 =$ _____

Name:_____ Date:_____

   Cross out and subtract.
Then, write the difference.

13
- 7

6

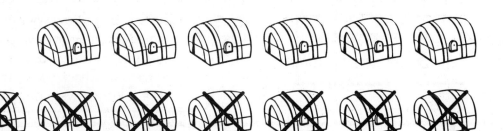

12
- 3

11
- 6

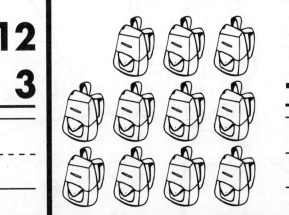

9
- 5

15
- 8

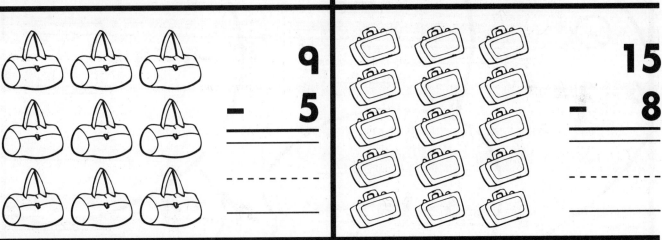

14
- 9

Name:_____ Date:_____

   Subtract and write the difference. Then, use the code to color the picture.

2 = orange	**4 = green**
3 = blue	**5 = yellow**

 Challenge: Draw your own picture. Insert your own subtraction equations and have a friend complete it. Check your friend's work to see if the answers are correct.

$$8 - 5$$

$$7 - 4$$

$$4 - 1$$

$$4 - 2 =$$

$$9 - 5$$

$$8 - 3 =$$

$$6 - 2 =$$

$$6 - 1 =$$

$$10 - 7$$

$$3 - 0$$

$$7 - 5 =$$

Name:_____   Date:_____

Review: Addition

  Add and write the sum.

```
  5       3       6       9       4       7
+ 6     + 9     + 7     + 4     + 3     + 2
____    ____    ____    ____    ____    ____


  8       2       9       8       7       5
+ 6     + 9     + 0     + 3     + 4     + 5
____    ____    ____    ____    ____    ____


  9       7       4       9       7       8
+ 5     + 7     + 4     + 6     + 3     + 8
____    ____    ____    ____    ____    ____


  4       8       7       9       5
  5       2       4       3       2
+ 3     + 3     + 3     + 3     + 3
____    ____    ____    ____    ____


  3       6       7       2       1
  3       6       1       6       5
+ 3     + 3     + 3     + 3     + 3
____    ____    ____    ____    ____
```

Name:_____   Date:_____

Review: Subtraction

  Subtract and write the difference.

10	11	14	13	18	16
- 7	- 6	- 5	- 3	- 8	- 2

12	10	9	13	11	8
- 9	- 5	- 7	- 8	- 7	- 5

10	14	8	15	13	18
- 6	- 8	- 6	- 6	- 5	- 9

11	12	14	12	15	10
- 2	- 4	- 6	- 8	- 7	- 8

17	13	16	11	9	12
- 7	- 6	- 6	- 9	- 5	- 7

 **TAKE A BREAK!** **You did a great job!**
Place your Book Mark here & RELAX!

Name:_____ Date:_____

  Count by 10's. Write how many in all.

_____

- - - - - - - - - -

_____

_____

- - - - - - - - - -

_____

_____

- - - - - - - - - -

_____

_____

- - - - - - - - - -

_____

_____

- - - - - - - - - -

_____

Count by 10's. Write the missing numbers.
Color the caterpillars.

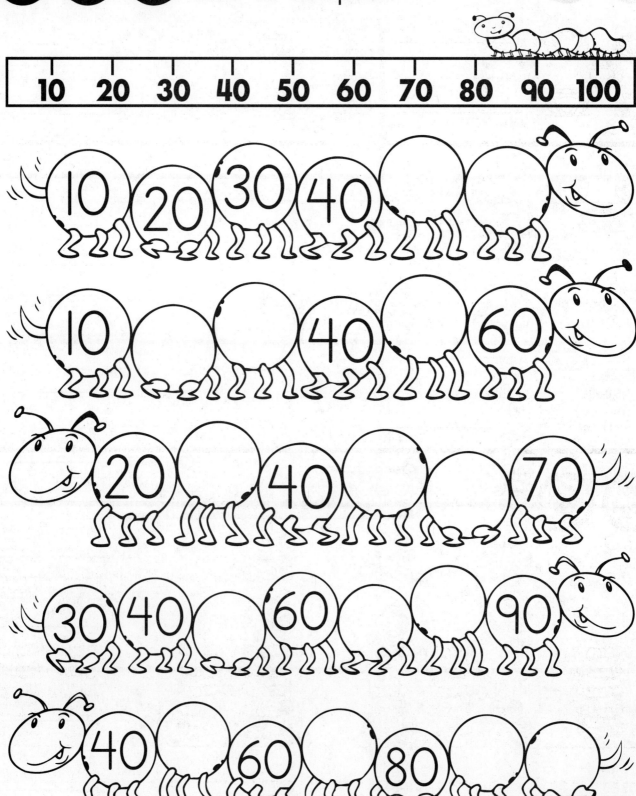

| 10 | 20 | 30 | 40 | 50 | 60 | 70 | 80 | 90 | 100 |

Counting and writing numbers by 10's

Count the frogs. Write how many in all.

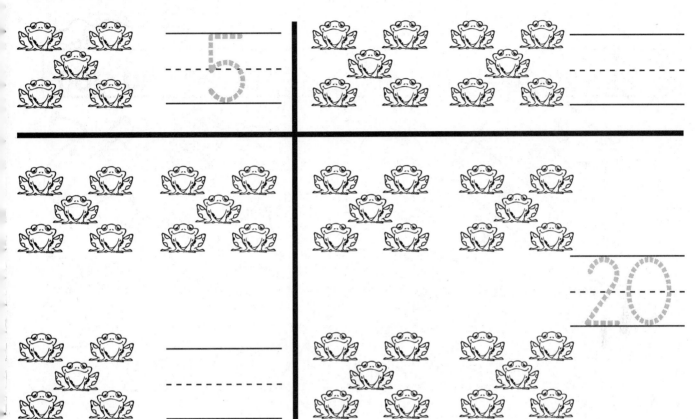

  Count by 5's. Write how many in all.

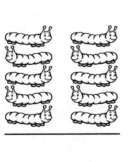

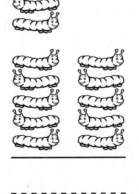

Color every fifth space red. Color the other spaces green.

1
2
3
4
5
6
7
8
9
10
11
12
13
14
15
16
17
18
19
20

Challenge: Continue writing the numbers from 21-100 on another piece of paper. Circle every fifth number. What pattern do you see with all the numbers you circled?

Count by 2's. Write the number to show how many items in all.

_____

- - - - - - - - - - -

_____

- - - - - - - - - - -

_____

- - - - - - - - - - -

_____

- - - - - - - - - - -

_____

- - - - - - - - - - -

Count by 2's to connect the dots from **2** to **20**.
Color the picture.

 Challenge: Can you make it all the way to 100, counting by 2's? Try it!

Counting by 2's; number order

Name:_____ Date:_____

   Read each story, add the numbers together, and write the sum.

Tip:
Write the numbers you are adding together above the answer line.

6 + 3 =

Rita sent **6** s.

Rob sent **3** ⬜ s.

How many ⬜ s in all?

_____
_ _ _ _ _ _ _ _
_____

Kate bought **8** 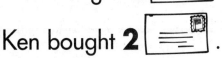 s.

Ken bought **2** .

How many ⬜ s in all?

_____
_ _ _ _ _ _ _ _
_____

Liz has **7** s.

Len has **0** ⬜ s.

How many ⬜ s in all?

_____
_ _ _ _ _ _ _ _
_____

Zack has **2** s.

Matt has **6** ⬜ s.

How many ⬜ s in all?

_____
_ _ _ _ _ _ _ _
_____

Name:_____   Date:_____

   Read each story, subtract, and write the difference.

Tip:
Draw pictures to show each problem. Cross out to find the answers.

There are five 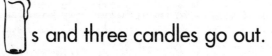s and four balloons blow away.

How many are left?   **5 – 4 =** _____

There are nine ⎕s and three candles go out.

How many are left?   **9 – 3 =** _____

There are ten 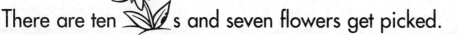s and seven flowers get picked.

How many are left?   **10 – 7 =** _____

There are eight 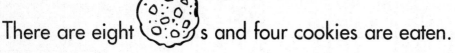s and four cookies are eaten.

How many are left?   **8 – 4 =** _____

There are seven s and two worms crawl away.

How many are left?

                 7 – 2 = _____

Name:_____   Date:_____

Review: Skip Counting

 Write the numbers to finish the chart.

1	2			5			8		10
11		13				17		19	20
21			24	25				29	30
31		33			36		38	39	
	42		44			47			50
51				55	56				60
61			64			67		69	
71		73			76				80
	82			85			88		90
91			94		96		98		100

      Count by 2's. Color those boxes yellow.
Count by 5's. Circle those numbers.
Count by 10's. Draw an X on those numbers.

Name:_____   Date:_____

Review: Addition & Subtraction Stories

   Read each story. Write a number sentence.
Add or subtract to solve, and write the answer.

There are **8** cats in the pet parade. Then, **2** more cats join the parade. How many cats are in the pet parade all together?

Tara bought **10** flowers. She bought **5** pansies and the rest were petunias. How many petunias did Tara buy?

_____

Serina has **2** goldfish in her bowl. Ray has **5** goldfish in his bowl. How many goldfish are there all together?

_____

Keisha picked **7** tomatoes from the garden. She used **5** tomatoes for a sauce and saved the rest for a salad. How many tomatoes did Keisha save?

_____

There are **6** horses in the barn. Then, **4** more horses are brought to the barn. How many horses are in the barn all together?

_____

Carlos picked **8** red apples and **5** green apples. How many more red apples than green apples did Carlos pick?

_____

STOP! TAKE A BREAK! You did a great job! Place your Book Mark here & RELAX!

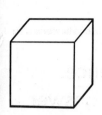 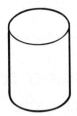 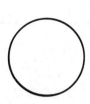 

cube   **cylinder**   **sphere**   **cone**

Challenge: Find an object in your house that looks like each of the following shapes: a **cube**, a **cylinder**, a **sphere**, and a **cone**.

 Draw a line to match each shape with the object that looks the same.

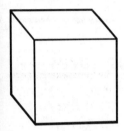

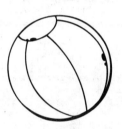

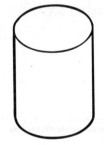

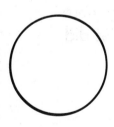

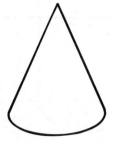

Draw the shape that comes next in each pattern. Color the shapes to make a pattern, too.

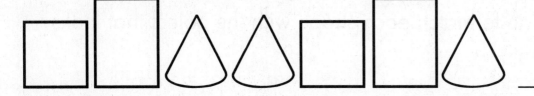

  Say the name of each shape. Then, draw lines, faces, dots, and colors to make a picture with the shapes below.

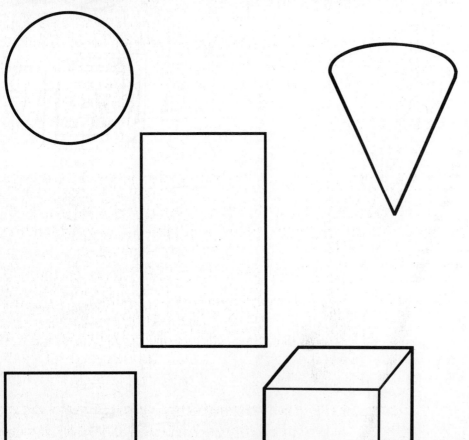

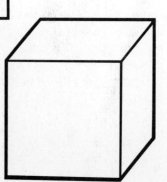

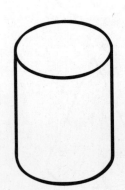

Name:_____   Date:_____

  Count each shape. Write how many.

How many   How many   How many   How many

□s? _____   ▭s? _____   ○s? _____   △s? _____

 Use the code to color the shapes.

□ = red   ▭ = yellow

○ = blue   △ = green

 Challenge: Play a *Shape Spotting* game at home. For example, say, "I spot something shaped like a cone." Then, have a family member try to guess the object with that shape. Take turns spotting different shapes.

Color the graph to show how many of each shape you counted on the previous page.

10				
9				
8				
7				
6				
5				
4				
3				
2				
1				

□   ○   △   ▭

Completing a graph

Name:_____ Date:_____

Review: Shapes

 Trace each 3-dimensional shape.

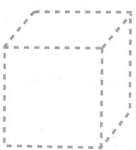         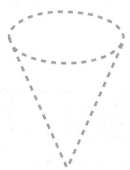

 Draw a picture of an object that is shaped like a **cube**.

 Color each **sphere** to show 3 kinds of balls used in sports.

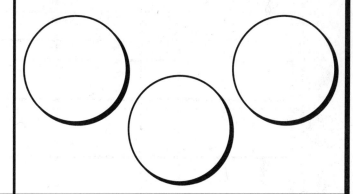

 Color each **cone** to show a different kind of party hat.

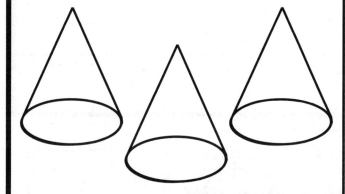

 Draw a food that might be packaged in a can shaped like a **cylinder**.

Name:_____ Date:_____

Review: Graphs

  Count how many the rabbit picked. Color the graph to show how many of each vegetable.

9					
8					
7					
6					
5					
4					
3					
2					
1					

STOP! **TAKE A BREAK!** **You did a great job!**
Place your Book Mark here & RELAX!

Review: Graphs

Circle the groups of ten. Write how many tens and ones. Then, write how many in all.

in all
2 tens + 4 ones = 24

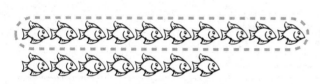

in all

____ tens + ____ ones = ____

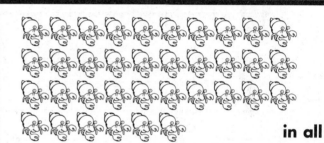

in all

____ tens + ____ ones = ____

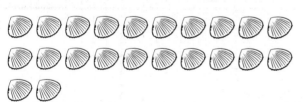

in all

____ tens + ____ ones = ____

in all

____ tens + ____ ones = ____

in all

____ tens + ____ ones = ____

in all

____ tens + ____ ones = ____

23
+   4
_____
27 in all

Tip:
Write the number 10 above each group of 10 blocks.

  Count the blocks. Write how many in all.

13 ⬜ ⬜⬜⬜
+   6 ⬜⬜⬜⬜⬜
_____
19 in all

24 ⬜ ⬜ ⬜⬜⬜⬜
+   2 ⬜⬜
_____
_____ in all

52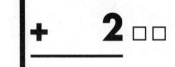
+   5 ⬜⬜⬜⬜⬜
_____
_____ in all

40 ⬜ ⬜
+   7 ⬜⬜⬜⬜⬜⬜⬜
_____
_____ in all

31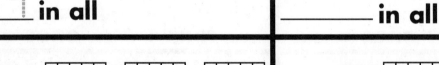
+   4 ⬜⬜⬜⬜
_____
_____ in all

63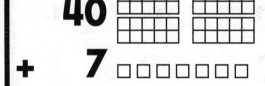
+   3 ⬜⬜⬜
_____
_____ in all

In Tenstown, everything comes in pack of 10.

tens	ones
3	0
+2	0
5	0

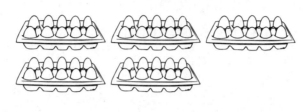

  First, add the ones together. Then, add the tens together. Write the sum.

tens	ones
4	0
+1	0
5	0

tens	ones
7	0
+2	0

$$\begin{array}{r} 30 \\ + 30 \\ \hline \end{array} \quad \begin{array}{r} 10 \\ + 70 \\ \hline \end{array} \quad \begin{array}{r} 40 \\ + 30 \\ \hline \end{array} \quad \begin{array}{r} 50 \\ + 20 \\ \hline \end{array} \quad \begin{array}{r} 60 \\ + 30 \\ \hline \end{array} \quad \begin{array}{r} 50 \\ + 40 \\ \hline \end{array}$$

$$\begin{array}{r} 60 \\ + 20 \\ \hline \end{array} \quad \begin{array}{r} 50 \\ + 30 \\ \hline \end{array} \quad \begin{array}{r} 80 \\ + 10 \\ \hline \end{array} \quad \begin{array}{r} 40 \\ + 20 \\ \hline \end{array} \quad \begin{array}{r} 10 \\ + 40 \\ \hline \end{array} \quad \begin{array}{r} 40 \\ + 40 \\ \hline \end{array}$$

First, subtract the numbers in the ones column. Then, subtract the numbers in the tens column. Write how many are left.

Tip: If there is not a number in the tens place, subtract zero (0).

tens	ones
3	5
−	3
3	2

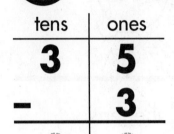

tens	ones
2	6
−	4

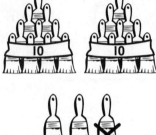

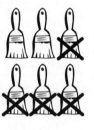

tens	ones
4	8
−	2

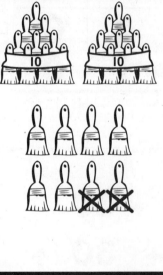

87	54	63	99	75
− 6	− 1	− 3	− 4	− 2

49	68	96	36	55
− 7	− 4	− 2	− 5	− 3

Subtract. Then, circle the correct answer.

```
    57            40
  -  2          - 10
  --------      --------
  59  (55)      20   30
```

```
    91            68
  -  0          -  6
  --------      --------
  91   90       64   62
```

```
    70            10            84            99
  - 20          - 10          -  3          -  3
  --------      --------      --------      --------
  50   90       10    0       82   81       96   95
```

```
    78            60            58            90
  -  5          - 10          -  2          - 60
  --------      --------      --------      --------
  74   73       50   70       54   56       20   30
```

Subtract. Then, use the code to color the picture.

8 = yellow	20 = red
12 = orange	30 = green

$$\begin{array}{r} 50 \\ -\ 20 \\ \hline \end{array}$$

$$\begin{array}{r} 70 \\ -\ 40 \\ \hline \end{array}$$

$$\begin{array}{r} 40 \\ -\ 10 \\ \hline \end{array}$$

$$\begin{array}{r} 18 \\ -\ 6 \\ \hline \end{array}$$

$$\begin{array}{r} 90 \\ -\ 60 \\ \hline \end{array}$$

$$\begin{array}{r} 80 \\ -\ 50 \\ \hline \end{array}$$

$$\begin{array}{r} 16 \\ -\ 8 \\ \hline \end{array}$$

$$\begin{array}{r} 19 \\ -\ 7 \\ \hline \end{array}$$

$$\begin{array}{r} 16 \\ -\ 4 \\ \hline \end{array}$$

$$\begin{array}{r} 13 \\ -\ 1 \\ \hline \end{array}$$

$$\begin{array}{r} 14 \\ -\ 2 \\ \hline \end{array}$$

$$\begin{array}{r} 30 \\ -\ 10 \\ \hline \end{array}$$

$$\begin{array}{r} 80 \\ -\ 60 \\ \hline \end{array}$$

Subtracting numbers without regrouping

Name:_____   Date:_____

Review: 2-Digit Addition

  Add. Color in the ◯ that shows the correct answer.

50 + **10** ◯40 ●60 ◯50	**23** + **41** ◯32 ◯64 ◯44	**60** + **3** ◯40 ◯63 ◯55
22 + **22** ◯44 ◯34 ◯22	**35** + **30** ◯65 ◯56 ◯45	**11** + **41** ◯62 ◯24 ◯52
80 + **0** ◯60 ◯80 ◯81	**74** + **3** ◯67 ◯71 ◯77	**30** + **20** ◯40 ◯60 ◯50
64 + **33** ◯94 ◯97 ◯93	**48** + **21** ◯96 ◯88 ◯69	**55** + **12** ◯67 ◯76 ◯43
94 + **5** ◯81 ◯91 ◯99	**34** + **34** ◯68 ◯34 ◯64	**78** + **11** ◯79 ◯89 ◯99

Name:_____ Date:_____

Review: 2-Digit Subtraction

  Subtract. Color in the ⬤ that shows the correct answer.

60 − 20	○ 60 ○ 50 ⬤ 40	
37 − 5	○ 32 ○ 31 ○ 30	
54 − 13	○ 42 ○ 41 ○ 40	

78 − 3	○ 76 ○ 75 ○ 74	
89 − 9	○ 90 ○ 81 ○ 80	
64 − 21	○ 48 ○ 45 ○ 43	

38 − 7	○ 32 ○ 31 ○ 30	
90 − 70	○ 30 ○ 20 ○ 10	
40 − 20	○ 30 ○ 20 ○ 10	

24 − 13	○ 37 ○ 11 ○ 31	
74 − 70	○ 10 ○ 4 ○ 8	
55 − 32	○ 23 ○ 33 ○ 43	

81 − 1	○ 90 ○ 80 ○ 70	
68 − 43	○ 52 ○ 26 ○ 25	
49 − 19	○ 20 ○ 30 ○ 40	

STOP! TAKE A BREAK! You did a great job! Place your Book Mark here & RELAX!

One shape can be divided into 2 **equal** parts OR 2 **halves** that are the same.

$$1 = \frac{1}{2} + \frac{1}{2}$$

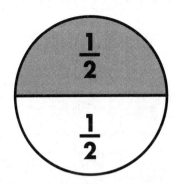

 Circle the shapes that show 2 equal parts or 2 **halves**.

 Color $\frac{1}{2}$ of each shape you circled.

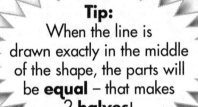

Tip:
When the line is drawn exactly in the middle of the shape, the parts will be **equal** – that makes 2 **halves**!

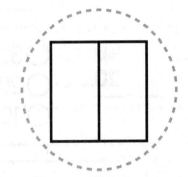

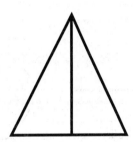

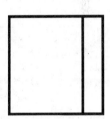

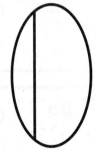

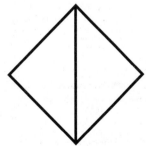

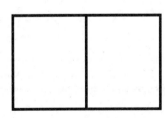

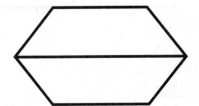

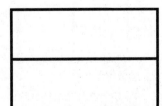

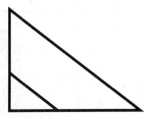

One shape can be divided into 4 **equal** parts OR 4 **quarters** that are the same.

$$1 = \frac{1}{4} + \frac{1}{4} + \frac{1}{4} + \frac{1}{4}$$

$\frac{1}{4}$	$\frac{1}{4}$
$\frac{1}{4}$	$\frac{1}{4}$

  Circle the shapes that show **quarters**. Color $\frac{1}{4}$ of each shape you circled.

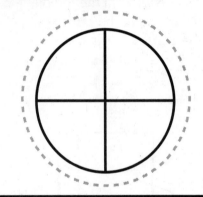

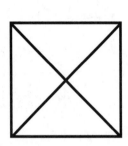

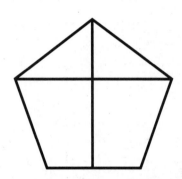

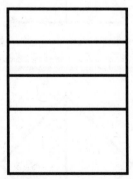

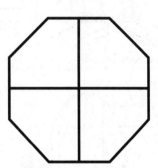

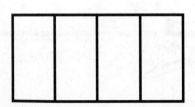

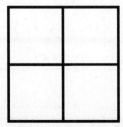

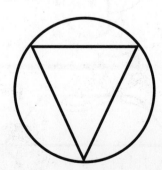

A **penny** is equal to one cent or **1¢**.

1¢ + **1¢** + **1¢** = **3¢**

> **Tip:**
> Look carefully to find only the **pennies** in each pocket. Cross out the coins that are not **pennies**.

    Color each **penny** brown. Count the **pennies** and write how many there are in each pocket.

_____ **pennies**

_____ **pennies**

_____ **pennies**

_____ **pennies**

 Challenge: Can you tell which pocket has the most **pennies**? Which has the fewest **pennies**? Color all the pockets.

A **nickel** is equal to **five cents** or **5¢**.

1 nickel
5¢

=

5 pennies
5¢

Color each **nickel** gray. Color each **penny** brown. Add the value of the coins together and circle the group that shows the largest value.

A **dime** is equal to **ten cents** or **10¢**.

  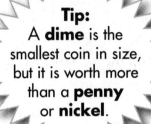

Tip:
A **dime** is the smallest coin in size, but it is worth more than a **penny** or **nickel**.

1 dime   =   10 pennies
10¢   10¢

  Add the value of the coins together. Write the total amount.

                ¢

     _____ ¢

    _____ ¢

   _____ ¢

   _____ ¢

A **quarter** is equal to **twenty-five cents** or **25¢**.

Challenge: Ask if you can count the change in your mom's purse or in your piggy bank. What is the total value of your coins?

1 quarter   =   **2 dimes + 1 nickel**
25¢   **25¢**

  Add to find the value of the coins in each purse. Color the purse if the value of the coins equals 25¢.

Name:_____   Date:_____

Review: Fractions

 Color $\frac{1}{2}$ of each fruit.

 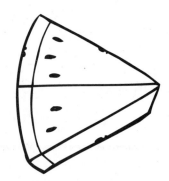 

 Color $\frac{1}{4}$ of each snack.

 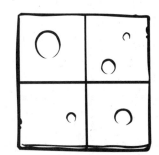 

  Color 1 part of each shape below. Is that equal to $\frac{1}{2}$ or $\frac{1}{4}$? Circle the correct answer.

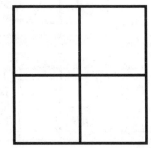 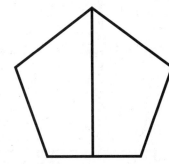 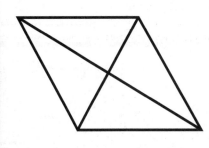

$\frac{1}{2}$ $\frac{1}{4}$ $\frac{1}{2}$ $\frac{1}{4}$ $\frac{1}{2}$ $\frac{1}{4}$

Name:_____ Date:_____

Review: Money

  Add the value of the coins. Write the total amount in the box.

25¢   **35¢**   **40¢**   **45¢**   **46¢**   **47¢**   [47]¢

25¢   35¢   45¢   50¢   ___¢   ___¢   [ ]¢

___¢   ___¢   ___¢   ___¢   ___¢   ___¢   [ ]¢

___¢   ___¢   ___¢   ___¢   ___¢   ___¢   [ ]¢

___¢   ___¢   ___¢   ___¢   ___¢   ___¢   [ ]¢

___¢   ___¢   ___¢   ___¢   ___¢   ___¢   [ ]¢

 TAKE A BREAK! You did a great job! Place your Book Mark here & RELAX!

Look at the measurement of each worm.
Write the length in **inches**.

about _____ inches

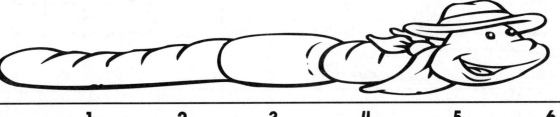

about _____ inches

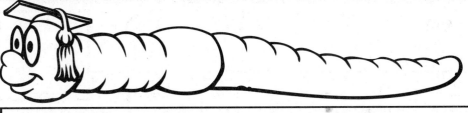

about _____ inches

about _____ inch

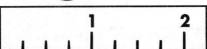

about _____ inches

Name:_____ Date:_____

  Look at the measurement of each object. Write the length in **centimeters**.

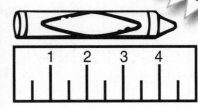

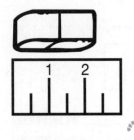

Tip:
Inches and **centimeters** are different measurements that are used in different parts of the world.

about _____2_____ **centimeters**

about _____ **centimeters**

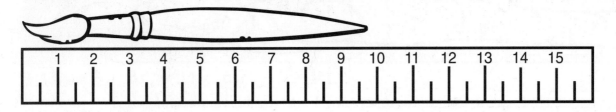

about _____ **centimeters**

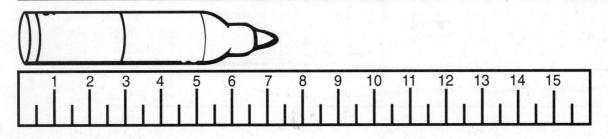

about _____ **centimeters**

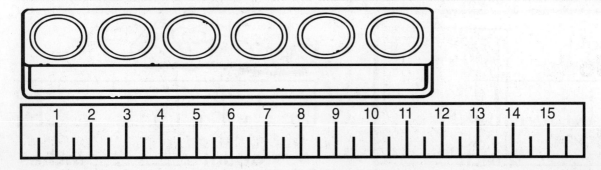

about _____ **centimeters**

The **minute hand** is on the 12.
The **hour hand** is on the 3.
It is 3 o'clock or 3:00.

  Look at the hands on each clock. Circle the correct time to the hour.

5:00

7:00

12:00

1:00

10:00

8:00

11:00

9:00

6 o'clock

7 o'clock

3 o'clock

2 o'clock

The **minute hand** is on the 6.
The **hour hand** is between the 8 and the 9.
It is eight-thirty or 8:30.

  Look at the hands on each clock. Circle the correct time to the half-hour.

9:30

8:30

1:30

11:30

8:30

7:30

5:30

6:30

three-thirty

two-thirty

four-thirty

five-thirty

Circle the name of the **month**.

 Draw an X on the squares that show the first and last **days** of the **month**. Draw a ▲ on each Wednesday of the **month**.

JULY

Sunday	Monday	Tuesday	Wednesday	Thursday	Friday	Saturday
		1	2	3	4	5
6	7	8	9	10	11	12
13	14	15	16	17	18	19
20	21	22	23	24	25	26
27	28	29	30	31		

 Challenge: What **month** is it right now? How many **days** are in the **month**? What is your birthday **month**? Can you name the 12 **months** of the **year** in order?

 Write the answers.

1. What is the first **day** of each **week**?_____

2. How many **days** are in one **week**?_____

3. How many Mondays are in this **month**?_____

4. What **day** of the **week** is July 10?_____

January   **February**   **March**   **April**
May   **June**   **July**   **August**
September   **October**   **November**   **December**

  Read each clue. Write the name of the **month**.

1. First month of the year   ____January____

2. Last month of the year   _____

3. Month after June   _____

4. Month before September   _____

5. Month between May and July   _____

6. Second month of the year   _____

7. Tenth month of the year   _____

8. Third month of the year   _____

9. Month between March and May   _____

10. Fifth month of the year   _____

11. Month before October   _____

12. Month before December   _____

Name:_____   Date:_____

Review: Measurement

   Look at the measurement of each fish.
Write the length in **inches** or **centimeters**.
Color all the fish.

 Challenge: Use a ruler to measure other items in **inches** or **centimeters:** a napkin, a pencil, a book, your foot, your dog's tail. Which is the longest and which is the shortest?

about _____ **inches**

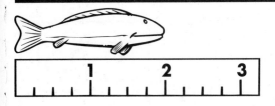

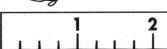

about _____ **inches**

about _____ **inch**

about _____ **centimeters**

about _____ **centimeters**

Name:_____ Date:_____

Review: Time

  Draw a line from each clock to the correct written time. Then, use the code to color the clocks and the fish.

| 1:00 = red | 8:30 = green | 4:30 = yellow | 9:00 = blue |

  eight-thirty  1:00

  1 o'clock  8:30

  four-thirty  9:00

  9 o'clock  4:30

 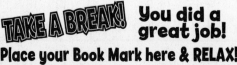 **TAKE A BREAK!** **You did a great job!** Place your Book Mark here & RELAX!

Answer Key

Please take time to review the work your child has completed and remember to praise both success and effort. If your child makes a mistake, ensure your child that it is all a part of learning and explain the correct answer, as well as how to find it. Taking the time to help your child shows your active interest in his or her learning process!

page 3

page 4
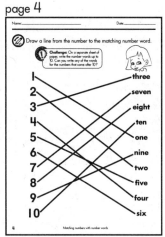

page 5
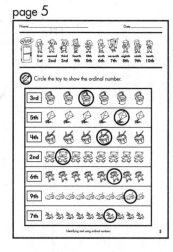

page 6
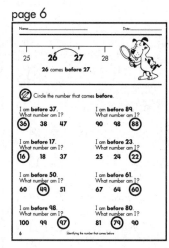

page 7
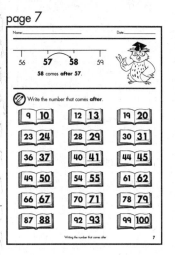

page 8
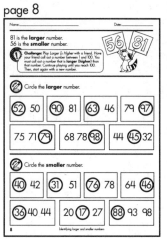

page 9
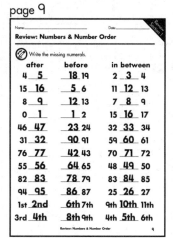

page 10
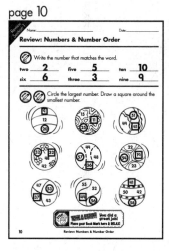

page 11

page 12
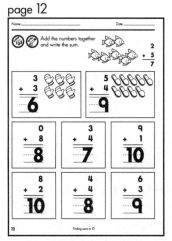

page 13

page 14

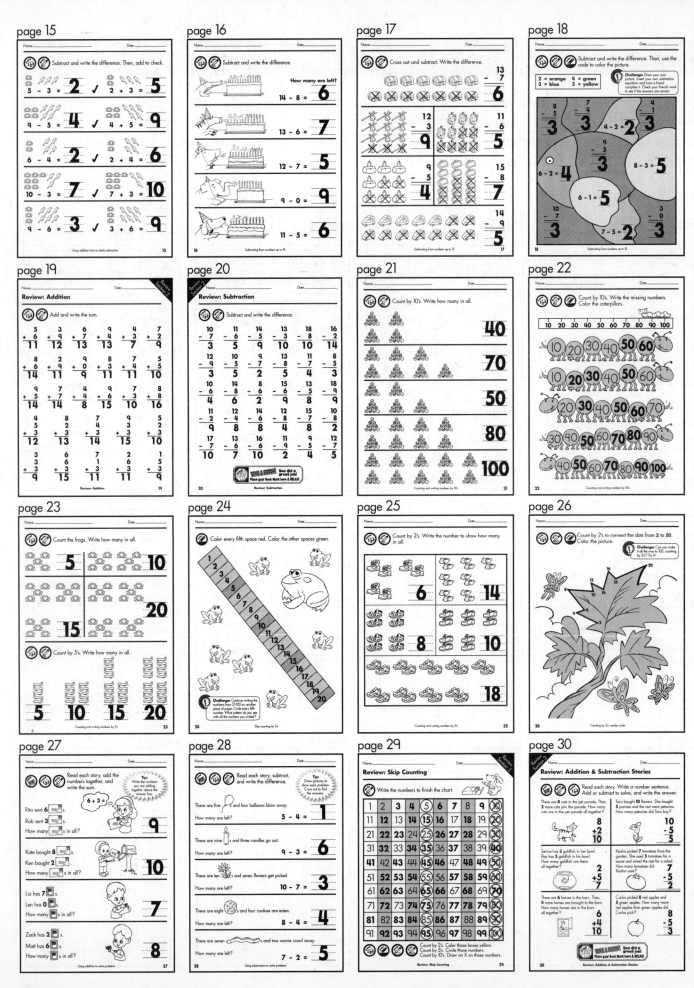

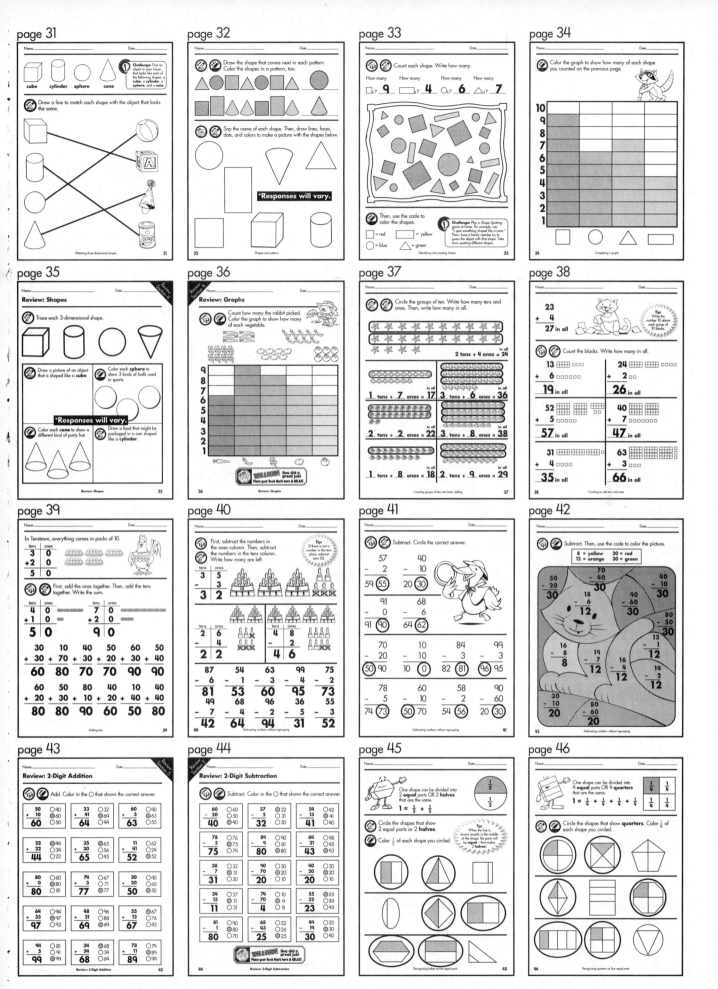

Answers

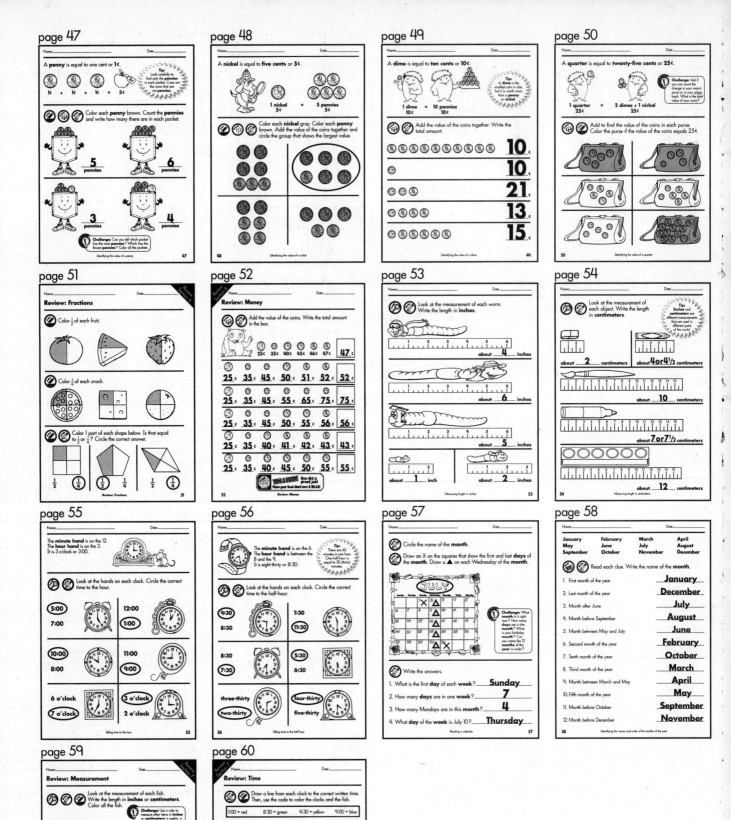

Answers

Find that Math Item Race!

1. Find a friend to play and a game piece (like a penny, a scrap of paper, or a small toy) & place it on the START space of your choice.
2. Take turns to see how quickly you can find each item on your path to the END space. When you find it, advance your game piece.
3. Play against a friend (or 2) to see who can get to the END first!
4. Switch START spots and play again!

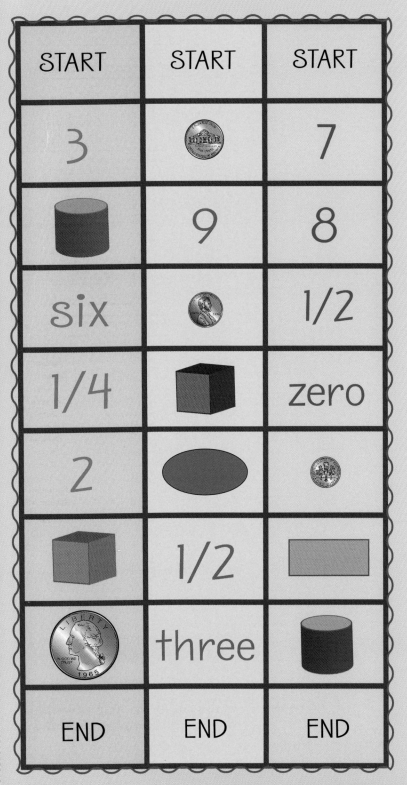

START	START	START
3		7
	9	8
six		1/2
1/4		zero
2		
	1/2	
	three	
END	END	END

_____'s

Your Name

Book Mark!

Tear out this Book Mark & use it to save your spot in the book.

Your Math Skills are totally nutty!

Take a break & come back to have more fun with numbers!

_____'s
Your Name

Skill Checklist!

HOO HOO!

Check off these skills as you practice them in the book:

- ☐ **Number Order & Words**
- ☐ **Ordinal Numbers**

- ☐ **Addition**
- ☐ **Subtraction**

- ☐ Skip Counting
- ☐ Word Problems

- ☐ Shapes
- ☐ Graphing

- ☐ **Two-Digit Equations**
- ☐ **Fractions**
- ☐ **Money**

- ☐ Length
- ☐ Time & Calendar

NUMBER RIDDLES WHO AM I?

I am the number of days in each week.
I come before eight and just after six.

Who am I?

I am the number of little pigs and blind mice.
I am also the number of sides on a triangle.

Who am I?

I am the number of sides on a stop sign.
I am also the number of arms on an octopus.

Who am I?

I am the number of states in the U.S. If you add the value of 5 dimes together, my number will be the answer.

Who am I?

I am the number of eggs in 1 dozen.
I am also the number of months in the year.

Who am I?

I am a 2-digit number and my digits are the same. I am the number just before 100.

Who am I?

I am larger than 70, but smaller than 80. If you add the value of 3 quarters together, my number will be the answer.

Who am I?

I am the number of minutes in 1 hour.
I am also the number you get if you add 30 + 30.

Who am I?

I am the number you find when you count all of your fingers and toes.

Who am I?

I am the number of sides on a square.
I am also the number of corners on a square.

Who am I?

I am the number before 18. My number is the same as the value of 1 dime and 7 pennies.

Who am I?

I am a number that you can find by skip counting by 10's. I am larger than 50 but smaller than 70.

Who am I?